APR 0 9

LAUGH <barcode> D0478434

MONUMENTAL MILESTONES
GREAT EVENTS OF MODERN TIMES

The Vietnam War

Left to right: President Lyndon B. Johnson, General Robert Ginsburg, and adviser Walt Rostow look at relief map of Khe Sanh area on February 16, 1968.

Mitchell Lane
PUBLISHERS

P.O. Box 196
Hockessin, Delaware 19707

Titles in the Series

MONUMENTAL MILESTONES
GREAT EVENTS OF MODERN TIMES

The Vietnam War

South Vietnamese soldiers on patrol for
Viet Cong soldiers.

Karen Bush Gibson

Copyright © 2008 by Mitchell Lane Publishers, Inc. All rights reserved. No part of this book may be reproduced without written permission from the publisher. Printed and bound in the United States of America.

Printing   1   2   3   4   5   6   7   8   9

Library of Congress Cataloging-in-Publication Data
Gibson, Karen Bush.
  The Vietnam War / by Karen Bush Gibson.
      p. cm. — (Monumental milestones)
  Includes bibliographical references and index.
  ISBN-13: 978-1-58415-541-6 (library bound)
  1. Vietnam War, 1961–1975—Juvenile literature. I. Title.
  DS557.7.G53 2005
  959.704'3—dc22

                                                                    2007000789

ABOUT THE AUTHOR: Karen Bush Gibson remembers seeing reports of the Vietnam War in newspapers and on television from when she was young. The news about the war affected her and motivated her to become a writer. Karen enjoys writing about people, places, and cultures for the juvenile educational market. Her published work includes *New Netherland: The Dutch Settle the Hudson Valley, Langston Hughes,* and *Mudslide in La Conchita, CA, 2005* for Mitchell Lane Publishers.

PHOTO CREDITS: p. 1—Yoichi R. Okamoto; p. 11—Library of Congress; p. 16—Malcom Browne; p. 22—PD-USGOV-MIL-NAVY; PD-USGOV-MILITARY-NAVY; p. 26—Jonathan Scott; p. 28, 33—Associated Press; p. 35—National Archives and Records Administration

PUBLISHER'S NOTE: This story is based on the author's extensive research, which she believes to be accurate. Documentation of such research is contained on page 46.

The internet sites referenced herein were active as of the publication date. Due to the fleeting nature of some web sites, we cannot guarantee they will all be active when you are reading this book.

                                                                              PPC

Contents

The Vietnam War

Karen Bush Gibson

*For Your Information

The U.S. Embassy in Saigon was one of several places attacked by North Vietnamese soldiers during the Tet Offensive on January 31, 1968.

Seven U.S. soldiers died trying to protect the embassy. Across South Vietnam, thousands more U.S., South Vietnamese, and North Vietnamese soldiers would die during the Tet Offensive— North Vietnam's most aggressive military campaign during the Vietnam War.

Surprise Attack

As many people lay sleeping in the Vietnamese city of Saigon during the dark early-morning hours of January 31, 1968, an explosion rocked the U.S. embassy in South Vietnam's capital city. A 3.5-mm bazooka rocket had blown a huge hole in the northern corner of the concrete wall surrounding the embassy. North Vietnamese and Viet Cong soldiers poured through the opening with guns sounding *rat-a-tat-tat*. Other enemy soldiers entered the embassy grounds with a storm of machine-gun fire, mowing down the U.S. Army military policemen guarding the gate.

Marine guards awakened Ambassador Ellsworth Bunker and placed him in the safest place they could find—a wine cellar five blocks away padded with pillows. At the embassy, more marines fought against the enemy, who were intent on gaining entrance into the building. Twenty-year-old Marine Corps guard Sergeant Ronald W. Harper later told reporters, "Explosions, bangs, thumps crashed all around me. I figured the VC [Viet Cong] were coming in. I slammed the heavy wooden embassy doors shut and as I did so a rocket, probably a 3.5-mm, hit the window and the side of the door, wounding my marine buddy in the arms, face and legs and throwing me to the ground."[1]

Colonel George Jacobson, who lived on the embassy grounds, was awakened by a shell hitting his window and sending shattered glass onto his bed. After six hours of fighting, the 716th Military Police Battalion came to the rescue, armed with grenades and M-16 automatic rifles. An impressed Jacobson watched from his second-floor window. "I saw them advance straight into the direction of enemy fire and silence that fire. If you want to get more brave than that, I would rather not be around."[2] The final tally at the embassy was seven U.S. soldiers dead, plus nineteen enemy soldiers.

Elsewhere in the city of Saigon, the sounds of war had blasted everyone awake. Before January 31, the noise of firing guns was muted as battles raged outside the city. Now the battles were happening *in* the city. The airport and the command post of the Seventh Air Force were hit hard. Viet Cong and North Vietnamese soldiers easily overtook the Saigon suburb of Cholon.

Five thousand troops attacked Saigon. It was common to see people coming to Saigon to celebrate the Tet holiday. But many of these people were actually soldiers disguised as farmers and peasants in the traditional loose-flowing black clothing that resembled pajamas. Others wore the white shirts of the professionals. All carried the curfew passes required of all civilians, although theirs were forged. Some North Vietnamese soldiers dressed as South Vietnamese soldiers had infiltrated the headquarters of the South Vietnam Joint General staff. Weapons were smuggled in separately. No one had any idea that troops were assembling right under their noses.

By afternoon of the first day, President Nguyen Van Thieu had declared martial law in Saigon.

Associated Press photographer Eddie Adams was driving around a ravaged Saigon with a cameraman from NBC that day. They came upon a sight they would never forget. General Nguyen Ngoc Loan, chief of the South Vietnamese national police, had captured a member of the Viet Cong. Dressed in black shorts and a checked shirt, the prisoner's hands were tied behind his back. Loan pushed the gun against the man's head and squeezed the trigger. "The man grimaced— then, almost in slow motion, his legs crumpled beneath him as he seemed to sit backward, blood gushing from his head as it hit the pavement."[3]

The North Vietnamese had taken the U.S. soldiers by surprise. The military had expected a couple of quiet days with a ceasefire in recognition of Tet, one of Vietnam's most important holidays. People celebrated the lunar new year and paid respect to their departed ancestors with feasting and fireworks.

What the South Vietnam and United States militaries didn't realize was that a well-planned attack was taking place in almost every major city and village. The attacks went off like firecrackers throughout twenty-six South Vietnamese towns in the early-morning hours, including the American complex at Cam Ranh Bay, and the mountain resort area of Da Lat. But no place was hit harder than the ancient provincial capital of Hue.

Hue was a beautiful city of temples, monuments, and palaces. It was considered sacred by many Vietnamese, particularly Buddhists. On this day, the Viet Cong attacked. They searched each house, killing people and taking prisoners. American Stephen Miller of U.S. Information Services was shot. A German doctor teaching medical school in Hue was found dead along with his wife and two other doctors. A Vietnamese priest, Father Bui Dong, was also killed. Americans still don't know exactly what happened in Hue that day. For years afterward, people would continue to find bodies just outside the city—three thousand bodies. Most had been shot or beaten to death, although signs indicated some might have been buried alive.

Journalist and writer Nguyen Qui Duc was a ten-year-old boy in Hue. His father hid his identification so that the enemy soldiers wouldn't know he worked for the government of South Vietnam. Nguyen and his mother watched helplessly as his father was taken anyway. "Between the bars of the window, I saw my father's silhouette. His arms were being tied behind his back and he was tied to other men in a file. . . . Then I saw the file of men marched away."[4]

In the days afterward, neither Nguyen nor his mother knew his father's fate: that he had been captured by the North Vietnamese. He was held prisoner for twelve long years. It would be even longer before Nguyen, who had moved to America, would see his father again. Nguyen's father had to wait four years after his release for permission to emigrate to the United States.

By afternoon of the first day of the Tet Offensive, the North Vietnamese and Viet Cong had raised their green and red flag with the yellow star at the highest point—the Citadel. The impressive structure was once the Imperial Palace, built by Emperor Gia Long in the early nineteenth century. The Citadel's walls were about twenty feet thick and thirty feet high, and were thought to be able to withstand almost any sort of attack.

Journalist H. D. Greenway, covering the Vietnam War for the *Washington Post* and *Time* magazine, was in Hue at the time. While standing next to a wall with some soldiers, one of the soldiers looked through an opening in the wall and was shot in the throat. Greenway and another soldier tried to carry the injured man away. Greenway explained, "Then a mortar or a rocket came and hit a lot of us and killed the guy we were carrying."[5]

U.S. Marine Captain Myron Harrington was with a group of marines that entered Hue. He reported coming into the desolate city where burned-out tanks sat on city streets next to the bodies of civilians. He and his men focused on the southeast corner of the Citadel. The North Vietnamese held on to the Citadel, blowing up the only access, a bridge across the Huong River. Inch by inch, both sides fought for territory. On February 25, the remaining North Vietnamese and Viet Cong troops sneaked out of the Citadel during the night. The South Vietnamese and U.S. soldiers won back Hue, but it had been devastated. Thousands of years' worth of culture and history were gone.

In Saigon, American and South Vietnamese soldiers quickly resumed control of most of the city. "Now, Americans saw a drastically different kind of war. The night before, nearly seventy thousand Communist soldiers had launched a surprise offensive of extraordinary intensity and astonishing scope,"[6] wrote war journalist Stanley Karnow.

Each side claimed victory. The United States won back the territory, but the North Vietnamese had proved they could shake up the U.S. military. Casualties were heavy on both sides—up to 7,000 U.S. and South Vietnamese soldiers were dead. Half a million civilians were left homeless. The North Vietnamese lost even more.

Back in the United States, the Tet Offensive changed people's perceptions of the Vietnam conflict, as it had often been called. This small Southeast Asian country was in the midst of a serious war, and the United States was heavily involved. As all eyes turned to Vietnam, it soon became apparent that this was a war no one could win.

Vietnam is a country in Southeast Asia with a rich and ancient culture. Although scientists have uncovered evidence of prehistoric cultures, recorded history began in 208 BCE when Chinese General Trieu Da conquered an area in the northern mountains populated by Viets, people of Mongolian heritage. Trieu Da established a country and called it Nam Viet. For hundreds of years, the Viets battled China for their independence. Two sisters by the name of Trung led one of the earliest revolts against Chinese rule. Another woman, Trieu Au, was known as the Vietnamese Joan of Arc as she fought for Vietnamese independence in the third century CE. The Vietnamese finally won independence from China in 939 CE, but battles

Chinese General Trieu Da

for control of the country continued. Warlords competed for ruling power for about thirty years, until the more stable dynasties of ruling families were established. During the 175-year Tran dynasty, the Vietnamese had to fight off Kublai Khan's armies. Chinese dynasties periodically invaded Vietnam and ruled, yet another Vietnamese dynasty would eventually overthrow the Chinese.

The first of the European traders came from ancient Rome to Vietnam, but it was Marco Polo's travels in Asia during the late-fourteenth century that stirred the interest of Europeans. Soon, European travelers were venturing to Asia for rich silks and jewels. One of the biggest treasures was the spices: cloves, nutmeg, and pepper were considered luxuries.

After land routes were established, Europeans began traveling to the Far East by ship. A Portuguese explorer, Antonio Da Faria, established a port city in Vietnam called Faifo, south of present-day Da Nang. Eventually, traders from throughout Europe were exploring Asia. Before long, Catholic missionaries traveled to Vietnam. A large number of Vietnamese embraced Christianity, and by the seventeenth century, Vietnamese priests were the leaders of the communities. In 1802, the fragmented country was united by Nguyen Anh of the Nguyen dynasty. As the first emperor, he became known as Gia Long and decided his country should be called Vietnam.

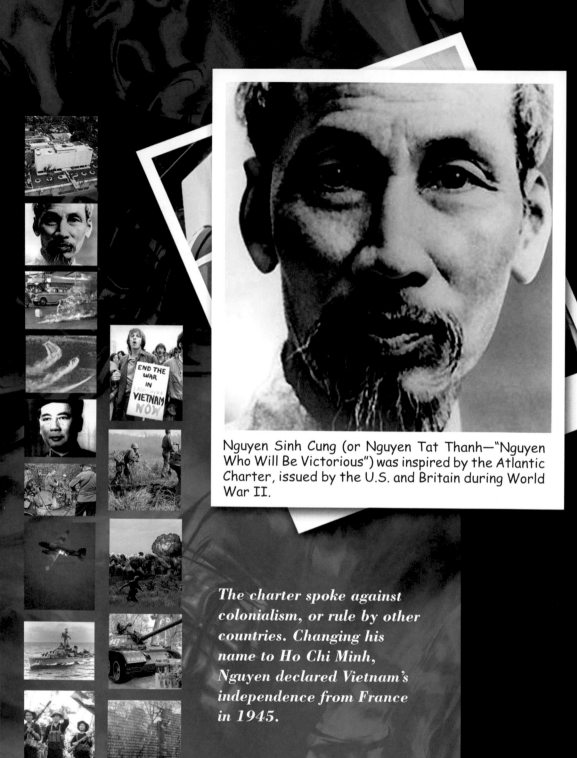

Nguyen Sinh Cung (or Nguyen Tat Thanh—"Nguyen Who Will Be Victorious") was inspired by the Atlantic Charter, issued by the U.S. and Britain during World War II.

The charter spoke against colonialism, or rule by other countries. Changing his name to Ho Chi Minh, Nguyen declared Vietnam's independence from France in 1945.

Vietnam Seeks Independence

The Southeast Asian peninsula, which includes Vietnam, is sandwiched between India and China. Together with the countries of Laos and Cambodia, the region became known as Indochina. Vietnam was a land of thick jungles, steep rugged mountains, and marshy areas. For foreigners, it was difficult terrain on which to fight a war.

France came to Vietnam's shores to stay during the 1800s, the era of colonialism. France, second only to Britain in number of colonies, took control of Indochina. Resistance to French rule grew over the years. As World War II developed, Vietnam found a new enemy in Japan, which invaded the country in 1940. The French hold on Vietnam began to crumble. When Japan surrendered on August 14, 1945, France tried to resume its rule—but nationalism was running high in Vietnam. After 100 years of colonial rule by France, the Vietnamese wanted an independent country.

An emerging leader voicing the need for Vietnamese independence was a man born as Nguyen Sinh Cung (or Nguyen Tat Tran according to some sources). As a young man, he toured the world and learned much about different countries and political systems. His primary goal was to unify Vietnam and rid the country of foreign powers. He decided the best route to do this was through the Communist Party. When he returned to Vietnam in 1941, he organized the Vietnamese to fight against Japan and France. The organization he started was called the Vietnam Doc Lap Dong Minh, or the Vietnam Independence League. Soon it became known as the Viet Minh. Along with the new organization, Nguyen Sinh Cung adopted a new name—Ho Chi Minh.

Ho Chi Minh was inspired by the Atlantic Charter, a statement issued by the United States and Britain that pushed for self-government for those countries that had been deprived of that right. "In the early days of World War II, American President Franklin Roosevelt and British Prime Minister

Winston Churchill inspired high hopes throughout the world that an Allied victory might bring an end to colonial domination,"[1] wrote historian Christian G. Appy. When the Viet Minh took the city of Hanoi from the French in 1945, Ho declared Vietnam's independence. He gave a speech in which he quoted America's Declaration of Independence, telling the crowd that "all men are created equal." The new country of the Democratic Republic of Vietnam (DRV) held elections, and Ho Chi Minh was chosen as president. The Viet Minh won more than 400 seats in the national assembly. North Vietnam soon formed alliances with the Soviet Union and China. These two Communist countries promoted the same ideas of sharing of work and property that North Vietnam practiced.

Ho Chi Minh hoped to have the support of the United States, as it also was once a colony that fought for its independence. The American Office of Strategic Services (OSS), a predecessor of the Central Intelligence Agency (CIA), had supported the Viet Minh's fight against the Japanese, yet withdrew from Vietnam when the Japanese surrendered in World War II. After that, help for fighting the French came from the Chinese. The Chinese provided Vietnam with modern weapons in their fight against the French.

Vietnamese troops under the command of General Vo Nguyen Giap advanced toward the mountainous French command post at Dien Bien Phu on March 13, 1954. According to the PBS special *Battlefield: Vietnam*, 3,000 French troops were killed, and another 8,000 troops were injured. Although the Vietnamese had even more casualties, France began questioning its presence in Vietnam. By the summer of 1954, both sides met in Geneva, Switzerland, to discuss peace.

Vietnam agreed to a temporary division at the seventeenth parallel during the Geneva Accords so that France could save its reputation. The north would be controlled by the Viet Minh, and the south by France and non-Communists. The plan was for the country to reunify during the 1956 national elections.

The U.S. government felt that the Geneva Accords gave too much power to Vietnam's Communist Party. This was the time of the cold war, when there were strong concerns about Communism in the Soviet Union and China. The United States encouraged the creation of the Southeast Asia Treaty Organization (SEATO) to form a democratic country in the south, known as the Government of the Republic of Vietnam (GVN).

Many non-Communists believed at the time that all Communists worked together. Actually, the Soviets and Chinese did not trust each other, and thousands of years of invasions by China had left Ho Chi Minh wary of Vietnam's enormous neighbor. For the most part, Ho played the countries against one another—China, the Soviet Union, France, and the United States.

A strongly vocal non-Communist, Ngo Dinh Diem, was named president of South Vietnam after a questionable election. Soon afterward, Diem claimed that the new country was in danger from the DRV, or North Vietnam, and asked for assistance from the United States. With the help of the CIA, thousands of Vietnamese were arrested. Diem passed laws that made it legal to hold someone in jail for suspicion of being a Communist. It soon became evident that Diem was a corrupt ruler, and many people began protesting against the South Vietnamese government. Diem stated that the protests were the work of Communists—and in America's eyes, Communism was a worse evil than government corruption.

In the mid-1950s, building began on a supply route along the Vietnam-Cambodia border. Later, the Ho Chi Minh Trail, as it was called, was used to move large numbers of North Vietnamese troops to South Vietnam. This set of roads and trails that weaved in and out of the Truong Son Mountains was a work in progress. Many of the workers were teenage girls. Laotian laborers and engineers from Russia, China, and North Korea also helped build the Ho Chi Minh Trail. By the end of the war, there would be more than 10,000 miles of trails.

The goal of the Communist Party of Vietnam prior to 1959 was to reunify Vietnam by political means. Believing that those methods had been ineffective, the Communist Party began using violence to overthrow Ngo Dinh Diem. They united with non-Communists against Diem in a group called the National Liberation Front (NLF). The U.S. government believed the NLF was really a Communist group. The military arm of the NLF became known as the Viet Cong, a term for Vietnamese Communists.

The United States responded by bringing in new equipment and more than 3,000 military advisers instructed not to engage in battles. Richard Olsen was one of those advisers: "Our main job was to fly South Vietnamese troops onto the field. We sometimes fired at targets from the air, but it was absurd because we're not allowed to shoot unless we were shot at."[2] Reports came from Vietnam about NLF victories, which led to Diem's government putting more pressure on the Vietnamese. Many people in the world who had never heard of Vietnam before were now seeing pictures in newspapers of Buddhist monks setting themselves on fire in protest of Diem's government.

Malcolm Browne finished his army tour in 1958 and returned to Vietnam as a journalist in 1961 for the Associated Press. He had been friendly with some of the Buddhists. On the evening of June 10, 1963, Browne was called about coming to a Buddhist temple at 7:30 the next morning. There, Browne saw something he would never forget. Young monks poured gasoline over an elderly monk, Thich Quang Duc. The gasoline covered the monk, who lit a match and dropped it in his lap. He was soon enveloped in flames.

"I just took photographs as fast as I could. It was not so much out of an urge to take pictures. As much as anything else it was to have something useful to do to keep my mind off this horrible spectacle. I'd never seen a man burn

To protest the Ngo Dinh Diem regime, several Buddhists monks set themselves on fire. Many felt the South Vietnamese government, led by Ngo Dinh Diem, was corrupt.

Journalist Malcolm Browne received a tip and caught the burning of a monk on camera. Soon after, South Vietnamese officials began confiscating photographs.

to death before,"[3] said Browne, who immediately sent the film to the AP bureau in the Philippines. Soon afterward, South Vietnamese officials began insisting that all film be developed before leaving Vietnam. Many photos were confiscated by the government.

The Vietnam terrain, thick with vegetation, provided easy places for the Viet Cong to wait to ambush troops. The United States began Operation Ranch Hand in 1962 to clear the vegetation on the sides of roads. This was done by spraying an herbicide nicknamed Agent Orange, which contained a dangerous chemical called dioxin. For ten years, Americans sprayed Agent Orange, destroying forests and crops. By 1971, increased cases of birth defects were being reported in Vietnam, and spraying stopped. Le Cao Dai, who ran the Agent Orange Victims Fund in Vietnam, was a doctor working in a jungle hospital during the war. He reported that most patients came to the hospital with non-combat-related problems. In 1966, the number of malaria cases increased dramatically; Le suspected these were linked to "some weakening of our immune systems caused by exposure to Agent Orange."[4]

Within nine years, increasing numbers of birth defects were reported. Health problems resulting from exposure to Agent Orange continue today for Vietnamese and U.S. soldiers exposed to the herbicide.

The U.S. began using Agent Orange to destroy some of the dense Vietnamese vegetation. Enemy soldiers would hide in these jungles before ambushing troops.

The first president of South Vietnam, Ngo Dinh Diem, was a corrupt leader.

Diem blamed the many protests against his government as the work of Communists and asked for help from the United States, who sent approximately 15,000 military advisers. Diem was arrested in a 1963 coup and later killed.

According to Browne, "In the early sixties the Americans were really waging a secret war, or at least a shadow war. The official line was that Americans were serving purely as advisers and only shooting at the Viet Cong in self-defense."[5]

The U.S. government did finally agree that Diem was out of control. Officials supported a 1963 coup by Diem's generals in the Army of the Republic of Vietnam (ARVN). Diem and his brother were captured on November 1, 1963, and later killed. However, the United States had more on its mind. Its own president, John F. Kennedy, was assassinated on November 22, 1963. At the time of Kennedy's death, the United States had 15,000 military advisers in Vietnam and had given $500 million in aid. The question was, what should the United States do now?

War correspondents have been following wars since the creation of newspapers. The earliest reporters sent their stories by telegraph. Newsreels of World War II were seen in movie theaters. Radio developed as another way to report the war. But Vietnam correspondents had new technology for reporting the war: television. The first televisions were introduced in the United States in 1936, but it was only after World War II that the industry began growing. Ten thousand televisions grew to six million by 1950. By the time U.S. troops were engaged in combat in Vietnam, over sixty million televisions sat in living rooms throughout the United States.

Each night on the evening news, people saw the war in Vietnam on their television screens. Many of the scenes were horrific: a marine using a cigarette lighter to burn down civilian huts; entire villages, including schools, churches, and hospitals, wiped out by U.S. bombs. As people began to see the war with their own eyes, they started questioning what their leaders were telling them. President Lyndon B. Johnson was said to be despondent on February 27, 1968, when respected newsman Walter Cronkite delivered his opinion

Walter Cronkite interviews Professor Mai of the University of Hue in 1968.

of the war: "It seems now more certain than ever that the bloody experience of Vietnam is to end in a stalemate. . . . It is increasingly clear to this reporter that the only rational way out then will be to negotiate, not as victors but as an honorable people who lived up to their pledge to defend democracy, and did the best they could."[6] It has been debated whether television influenced public opinion regarding the war or whether it simply provided other viewpoints.

Newspapers remained an important source of information about the war, too. During World War II, Congress passed laws banning the publication of any material that could interfere with the war effort or harm national security. The same concerns led the government to try to stop the *New York Times* and the *Washington Post* from publishing a secret study of the Vietnam War. The Supreme Court ruled that the newspapers could indeed print the study, which was called the Pentagon Papers.

U.S. military pilots waged an air war over North Vietnam with planes like the AC-47.

Also known as Spooky or Puff, this side-firing attack cargo plane carried 16,500 rounds of ammunition. The United States provided many of the weapons used by the South Vietnamese during the Vietnam War.

Americans Join the War in Vietnam

Flying from the United States to Vietnam takes over thirty hours, with typical stops in Anchorage, Alaska; Seoul, South Korea; and Hong Kong. It was a long way to go to fight a war—but that's exactly what seven million Americans did over a ten-year period.

Immediately after New Year's Day in 1963, the Viet Cong ambushed the South Vietnamese army at the village of Ap Bac. Although armed with American weapons, almost 400 South Vietnamese soldiers were killed or wounded. Three American advisers were also killed.

By the next year, America had arrived with airplanes. It is said that two wars were fought in Vietnam—the ground war in South Vietnam and the air war over North Vietnam—and it was in the air that the Americans excelled. According to Appy: "Every day for more than a decade the skies over Vietnam were filled with a myriad of lethal aircraft, from the AC-47 'Spooky' gunships that fired eighteen thousand machine gun rounds a minute, to the A-1 Skyraiders that swooped down to the treetops to release 150-gallon canisters of napalm, to the B-52 Stratofortresses that were capable of dropping twenty-seven tons of bombs from six miles high."[1]

Most of the fighter jets and bombers came from aircraft carriers operating in the Gulf of Tonkin. This body of water between Vietnam and China played a significant role in America's participation in the Vietnam War. It was a dark and eerily quiet night on July 30 when South Vietnamese commandos attacked two small North Vietnamese islands in the Gulf of Tonkin. As North Vietnamese boats rushed to the aid of those on the islands, the USS *Maddox* received orders to simulate an air attack. From 123 miles away, this destroyer

The USS *Maddox* (above) and the *C. Turner Joy* were just two of the U.S. ships that patrolled the Gulf of Tonkin.

After the USS Maddox was hit by the North Vietnamese, Congress passed the Gulf of Tonkin Resolution. The resolution gave President Johnson the power to take action in Southeast Asia.

spy ship was able to divert the attention of the North Vietnamese from the commandos. The USS *Maddox* received a minor hit, and President Johnson ordered U.S. forces to retaliate against the North Vietnamese. American fighter jets bombed two naval bases and a major oil facility.

On August 4, President Johnson delivered a speech on television telling the American public that in addition to attacking peaceful South Vietnamese villages, the North Vietnamese had committed two acts of aggression against two American ships, the USS *Maddox* and the *C. Turner Joy*. Almost unanimously, Congress passed the Gulf of Tonkin Resolution three days later, giving the president the power to take whatever actions he believed were necessary to defend Southeast Asia.

Later, the captain of the USS *Maddox* said there had been no second attack against the ship. Yet events steamrolled ahead because of the incident.

The new resolution allowed the president to engage the U.S. military in Vietnam without a formal declaration of war from Congress. Significant debate on the best course of action to take in Vietnam was the focus of the administration. Some wanted to increase U.S. troops and take a more aggressive stance. Others wanted to proceed cautiously. A few government officials were already wondering if the United States should pull out of Vietnam altogether. Days before Lyndon B. Johnson was reelected president of the United States, the Viet Cong attacked Bien Hoa Air Base near Saigon. Mortar shells killed four Americans, injured seventy-six, and destroyed five B-57 bombers.

In early 1965, the Viet Cong seemed to grow in strength as they launched numerous attacks throughout South Vietnam, killing civilians and soldiers, Americans and South Vietnamese. When a U.S. helicopter base was attacked, President Johnson ordered U.S. Navy fighters to bomb North Vietnam. The Viet Cong responded by bombing a hotel in Qui Non, killing twenty-three Americans. Then the U.S. military put Operation Rolling Thunder into effect. The three-and-a-half-year plan was to bomb North Vietnam until it stopped helping Viet Cong forces in the south. American pilots attempted to derail North Vietnam's transportation system by bombing roads, bridges, and supply depots.

Operation Rolling Thunder ended on November 1, 1968, with significant losses on both sides. The Americans lost more than 900 aircraft, and 818 pilots were dead or missing. Many who survived being shot down became prisoners of the North Vietnamese. The United States estimated that Operation Rolling Thunder cost North Vietnam more than 200,000 civilians and Chinese support personnel.

When North Vietnam refused to sign a peace agreement with the United States, President Johnson ordered the first American combat troops to Vietnam. They were joined by Allied forces from Korea and Australia. In response, the Viet Cong changed its strategy. They knew they could not defeat a superior military power like the United States, so instead they planned for a long and drawn-out war.

North Vietnamese and Viet Cong forces began using guerrilla tactics learned from the Chinese. In guerrilla warfare, a fighting force (such as the

North Vietnamese) that is outmatched in terms of conventional weapons uses the element of surprise and unfamiliar, difficult terrain to their advantage. In Vietnam, guerrilla tactics included hiding the bases where training and war strategy took place. Some bases were located in isolated swamps or forests, hidden from American planes.

Viet Cong leaders required villagers to dig three feet of tunnel a day. Only twenty miles from Saigon, nearly 200 miles of tunnels lay underneath the Cu Chi base. Guerrillas traveled through trapdoors and secret entrances to the network of tunnels in the National Liberation Front areas.

For the United States, the Vietnam War could no longer remain a secret conflict. There were not enough troops to fight the quickly escalating war, so the government enacted a military draft from the draft-eligible males registered with the Selective Service System.

President Johnson appointed General William Westmoreland as commander of U.S. forces in Vietnam in 1964. He planned to win the war by protecting U.S. bases in South Vietnam, while sending troops to the central highlands to block North Vietnam. He also wanted to launch "search-and-destroy" operations and intense bombing. On June 27, 1965, he ordered the first offensive operation on land by American forces northwest of Saigon. Operation Starlite was the first major battle of the war. Ground, air, and sea troops successfully joined forces to kill 700 Viet Cong soldiers.

Fighting continued in small towns throughout South Vietnam, and both sides suffered heavy casualties. The United States deployed almost 8,000 troops in early 1966 with the intention of capturing the Viet Cong headquarters in Saigon, but the headquarters was never located.

The area around the border separating North and South Vietnam was a demilitarized zone, or DMZ for short. Although this area was neutral, a three-week-long battle occurred there in May 1966. U.S. Marines and South Vietnamese troops drove the North Vietnamese back, and throughout the summer North Vietnam suffered heavy casualties. When it looked as if the war might finally be turning in South Vietnam's favor, reinforcements arrived from the Ho Chi Minh Trail. The Viet Cong depended on the Ho Chi Minh Trail for weapons, ammunition, and special equipment.

The Viet Cong were successful with guerrilla warfare. They used an amazing system of underground tunnels to travel undetected.

Viet Cong, or Vietnamese Communists, were soldiers who belonged to the National Liberation Front.

Although wary of each other, the Chinese government supplied the Viet Cong with Chinese and Soviet machine guns; the most popular was the Chinese version of the Soviet AK-47 submachine gun. The Viet Cong also used rocket-propelled grenades, recoilless rifles, and mortars. The Russian-built MiG-21 was a superior weapon also favored by the North Vietnamese. This supersonic fighter aircraft was used in high-speed hit-and-run attacks.

By the end of 1966, approximately 391,000 American soldiers were based in Vietnam and offshore. In one year, more than 6,000 Americans had been killed. Five times that amount had been wounded, many seriously. Even more Viet Cong had died, yet the casualties didn't affect the continued aggression by Viet Cong and North Vietnamese soldiers.

When 1967 came, the North Vietnamese concentrated on bombing American bases in the DMZ. Thirty thousand U.S. and South Vietnamese forces

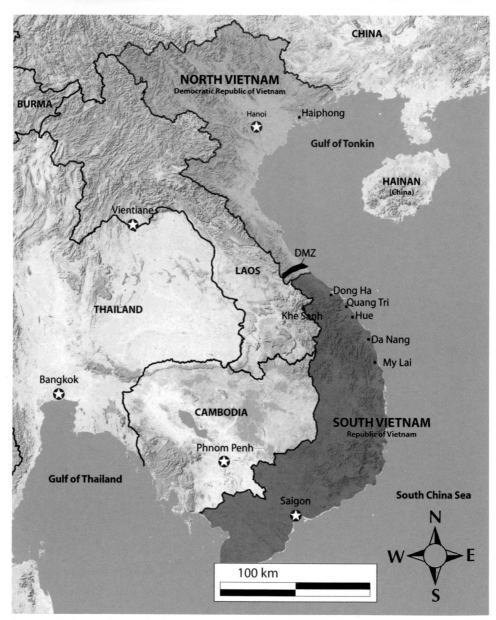

Located along the Indochina coast, Vietnam is a long narrow country covered by marshes and jungles. During the Vietnam War, the country was divided into North and South Vietnam, with the U.S. fighting on the side of South Vietnam. Once the war ended, the country was no longer divided. Hanoi became the capital of the unified Socialist Republic of Vietnam.

Viet Cong leaders forced villagers to make weapons and booby traps out of spare parts. Much of the metal came from parts of American weapons; more came from scraps like tin cans.

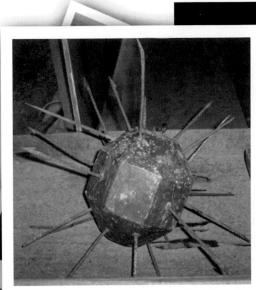

Waiting in the jungle treetops, Viet Cong soldiers lobbed these spiked weapons at U.S. soldiers.

moved into a sixty-square-mile area known as the Iron Triangle bordered by the Saigon River. Snipers, ambushes, and booby traps accounted for many deaths at the hands of the North Vietnamese. Army nurse Sylvia Lutz Holland served from 1968 to 1969 at the 312th Evacuation Hospital in Chu Lai. She reported seeing a lot of men who had stepped on land mines. "It was a guerrilla war and the whole idea was not to kill but to maim and injure and decrease morale."[2]

Villagers made many of the booby traps and land mines from everyday items like tin cans and wire. The explosives came from American bombs thought to be duds scattered throughout the countryside. Many children were asked to help with the traps.

Vietnamese civilians suffered the most. Both the South Vietnamese army and the Viet Cong frequently tortured peasants to get information or to punish them for siding with the enemy. In 1962, South Vietnamese officials

A U.S. soldier patrols for survivors after the siege at Khe Sanh, a remote U.S. base.

In January of 1968, North Vietnamese soldiers launched an attack that would last seventy-seven days and would become one of the fiercest battles of the Vietnam War.

had begun building "strategic hamlets." These government villages, surrounded by barbed wire, kept the Viet Cong from having access to the villagers. For their part, villagers were angry at being taken from their homes.

In late April 1967, Americans began attacking North Vietnam's airfields. Many North Vietnamese air bases were hit. Battles took to the skies as American pilots shot down twenty-six North Vietnamese jets over Hanoi.

In January 1968, North Vietnamese forces gathered near an isolated U.S. Marine base at Khe Sanh. In the first two days, they launched over 1,300 artillery rounds at the base, killing eighteen marines. For eleven weeks, the North Vietnamese fired upon the base, while the Americans responded with heavy bombing. Finally, the United States proved victorious in the longest battle of the Vietnam War, in which 1,600 North Vietnamese lost their lives. With no more need for the base, General Westmoreland gave orders for Khe Sanh to be destroyed.

Constant images on television and situations like the Tet Offensive put the Vietnam War on everyone's mind. Young men were being drafted, and some were not returning home alive. Some young men of draft age refused to serve in the military because they were against the war. Some of them went to Canada to live; others went to prison. One of the most famous people who refused to serve was a heavyweight boxer named Cassius Clay. He later adopted the Muslim name of Muhammad Ali.

Antiwar sentiment continued growing in America, leading to frequent protests in major cities and college campuses. Modeled after the civil rights movement, the anti-war movement worked for change mostly through peaceful protests. But like some of the civil rights protests, sometimes violence happened anyway.

Two of the most well-known protests against the Vietnam War were at the Chicago Democratic Convention in 1968 and Ohio's Kent State University in 1970. Speculation at the convention on who would be chosen to run for president was especially high, because Lyndon B. Johnson had decided not to seek re-election. Antiwar protesters thought it was a good time to let politicians know how they felt. Hundreds of thousands of people descended on Chicago to protest against America's

Vietnam war protesters in the United States

role in the Vietnam War. As antiwar demonstrators advanced to where the convention was being held, police and National Guardsmen began chasing and attacking the audience, which was made up largely of young adults. Riot police used clubs and tear gas to subdue demonstrators before arresting hundreds.

At the end of April 1970, President Richard Nixon ordered a major bombing campaign in the country of Cambodia, next to Vietnam. The decision sparked a large number of protests on college campuses. During the protest at Kent State University on May 4, the Ohio governor ordered the National Guard to the campus to restore order. Guardsmen fired at the students, killing four and wounding nine. Sometimes antiwar protests led to the violence that people were protesting against.

U.S. troops fighting in Vietnam found it difficult to maneuver and even find the enemy because of the thick undergrowth of the country.

Using guerrilla warfare tactics, the Viet Cong often hid booby traps and land mines in the brush. A large number of U.S. soldiers were maimed just by taking a wrong step.

How to End a War

Soon after the Tet Offensive, Lyndon B. Johnson announced that he would not seek reelection. Some said President Johnson made this decision because of poor health (he died in early 1973). Others thought the direction in which the Vietnam War was heading had a lot to do with Johnson's decision. During his terms, more than 500,000 troops were sent to Vietnam, and U.S. air attacks had also increased. Secret negotiations began in Paris in the spring of 1968 between the Americans and the North Vietnamese, although the negotiations did not stay secret for long.

Meanwhile in Vietnam, the fighting continued. Many men watched friends and fellow soldiers lose their lives to booby traps and snipers. Infantrymen from Charlie Company advanced on the village of My Lai on March 16, 1968, and killed approximately 200 civilians. The dead ranged from the very young to the very old. According to journalist Seymour M. Hersh's account, "suddenly there was a burst of automatic fire from many guns. Only a small child survived. Somebody then carefully shot him, too."[1]

U.S. policy had always been to protect civilians, but for some reason some of the men in this troop killed these civilians. It is unclear why. The official report stated that 128 Viet Cong had been killed. American military and freelance journalists aware of the incident spent a year trying to get the truth to people. The truth finally came out when the December 5, 1969, issue of *Life* magazine showed graphic photos of the My Lai massacre that included bodies of the victims. The news of what really happened at My Lai was unsettling to other U.S. soldiers and Americans back home. Twenty-five officers and enlisted men were charged with the killings at My Lai or with covering them up. The platoon leader, Lieutenant William Calley, was found guilty at a military court in Fort Benning, Georgia.

In November of 1968, Americans elected Richard M. Nixon as president. He promised "peace with honor" through the negotiation for the withdrawal of half a million troops in a way that allowed South Vietnam to function as an autonomous country. Nixon's plan dictated that the South Vietnamese armies would be responsible for the ground war and the U.S. military for the air war. By the time he took office, 30,000 Americans had died in Vietnam.

In March of 1969, President Nixon ordered the bombing of North Vietnamese and Viet Cong bases located in Cambodia. Cambodia was devastated by the onslaught of bombs over the next few years. In the same month, North Vietnamese and Viet Cong attacked towns, cities, and U.S. bases throughout South Vietnam. Saigon took some shattering blows, but eventually American air raids drove the Viet Cong back.

President Nixon and South Vietnamese President Nguyen Van Thieu met on Midway Island on June 8, 1969. They announced that 25,000 American troops would be withdrawn immediately from Vietnam. Meanwhile, a peace agreement had been drafted in the Paris peace talks by U.S. Secretary of State Henry Kissinger and North Vietnamese representatives. Thieu refused to support the agreement.

Meanwhile, the health of the beloved leader of the North Vietnamese, Ho Chi Minh, was poor. His heart had been failing for months and by August of 1969, he was no longer able to work. He died September 3. The death of the man many knew as "Uncle Ho" caused widespread mourning and a promise by North Vietnamese leaders to finish what Ho Chi Minh had started.

After Nixon's first year in office, an additional 10,000 Americans had died in Vietnam. It didn't look as though peace would come anytime soon. South Vietnamese troops pushed into Cambodia on April 29, 1970, searching for Viet Cong bases. President Nixon ordered more bombings. By May 1, three U.S. divisions had attacked Cambodia, with the fighting lasting for sixty days. A huge supply of weapons was discovered, including sixteen million rounds for small arms. The Viet Cong lost 10,000 men, but still were not deterred. "On the whole, Vietnamese culture is tougher than ours. I saw Vietnamese kids with bullet holes in their legs who didn't complain,"[2] said American pilot Richard Olsen.

Perhaps hoping for a similar success, the South Vietnamese armies moved into the nearby country of Laos to attack two known Viet Cong bases. Instead, they walked into a trap. Nine thousand South Vietnamese troops were killed or wounded.

Meanwhile in America, leaders felt the pressure to get Americans out of Vietnam, especially after the Pentagon Papers were published in the *New York Times* in 1971. With strong antiwar feelings, Department of Defense aide Daniel Ellsberg had made a copy of secret Vietnam War documents and released them to the press. One bit of information that came out was that the United States had been involved in secret operations in Vietnam long before the Gulf of Tonkin Resolution—operations that "had become so extensive by August 1964 that Thai pilots flying American T-38 fighter planes apparently bombed and strafed North Vietnamese villages near the Laotian border on Aug. 1 and 2."[3]

Napalm is so thick that it sticks to and burns surfaces, including skin. People hit with napalm either suffer greatly with severe second-degree burns or die from third-degree burns.

Some of the weapons that the United States used in Vietnam were bombs made from jellied gasoline, called napalm bombs.

By the end of 1971, two-thirds of American troops had been withdrawn from Vietnam. Allied troops were also leaving. Over a million South Vietnamese soldiers fought the war on the ground with the help of only 133,000 U.S. soldiers. On May 19, 1971, the last of the Allied Australian troops had withdrawn from Vietnam.

On March 30, 1972, more than 20,000 North Vietnamese troops crossed the DMZ and forced the South Vietnamese army back. The North Vietnamese pushed on to the city of Hue and took control of the northern part of the city. It took 4,000 South Vietnamese soldiers aided by American B-52 bombers to force Viet Cong troops to withdraw about six weeks later. Meanwhile, North Vietnamese forces took two other towns, Quang Tri City and Dong Ha, in the Binh Dinh province.

The Americans and North Vietnamese had continued with peace talks in Paris, but by mid-December talks had broken down. President Nixon ordered air strikes against North Vietnam airfields, transportation targets, and supply depots. More than 20,000 tons of bombs were dropped around North Vietnam's largest cities of Hanoi and Haiphong. These attacks, named the Christmas bombings, brought immediate disapproval from the world. President Nixon knew he had to reconsider negotiation. Peace talks resumed on January 8, 1973. Three weeks later, all sides agreed to a cease-fire.

The last American combat soldiers left Vietnam on March 29, 1973. Military advisers and marines protecting American bases remained. For the United States, the war was officially over. Of the more than three million American soldiers who had served in the Vietnam War, almost 58,000 were killed and 150,000 were seriously wounded. More than 1,000 U.S. soldiers were missing in action, possibly prisoners of war.

Prisoners have been a part of war for hundreds of years. Although it was America's longest war, the Vietnam War had fewer American prisoners of war (POWs) than previous wars. About 800 American POWs were in Vietnam, compared to 7,000 in Korea and 130,000 in World War II. Yet the circumstances of the Vietnam POWs were every bit as harrowing. According to the organization Nam-POW, the average length of time as a prisoner was twelve years. Over half the POWs were held in North Vietnam. Others were imprisoned in South Vietnam camps, Laos, Cambodia, and China. Former U.S. Navy pilot Porter Halyburton was imprisoned for eight years. When he refused to cooperate with his captors, they kept moving him to far worse places. When U.S. forces bombed Hanoi in 1966, he and sixty others were marched through the streets, where people threw things at them. He and many others endured torture. Yet many POWs reported that one of the hardest things about being a POW wasn't the torture, but the isolation from other prisoners.

Some American soldiers were listed as MIA, or missing in action. During the 1970s, POW bracelets were sold in the United States with the names of POW and MIA servicemen to bring awareness to the situation. At the end of the Vietnam War, there reportedly were 2,583 Americans unaccounted for. Due to this high number and reports from other sources, there was concern that there may have been live prisoners

American servicemen, former prisoners of war, are cheering as their aircraft takes off from an airfield near Hanoi as part of Operation Homecoming, February 1973.

remaining in Vietnam. Senator John McCain, himself a Vietnam veteran and former POW, pushed a bill through Congress called the McCain Bill (Public Law 102-190). The law declares that Department of Defense documents related to people still unaccounted for should be made available for public viewing. As a result, a POW/MIA database was compiled. According to the National League of Families of American Prisoners and Missing in Southeast Asia, as of October 29, 2005, there were still 1,815 people unaccounted for.

April 1975

After American troops were pulled from Vietnam in 1973, the war lingered for a couple of years. On the morning of April 30, 1975, the North Vietnamese Army entered Saigon and advanced toward the presidential palace.

END THE WAR IN INDO-CHINA VIETNAM NOW

As this group of soldiers (inset) drove Tank 843 through the palace gates, Saigon fell, and the South Vietnamese government surrendered. Saigon was renamed Ho Chi Minh City.

CHAPTER 5

Aftermath

The Paris peace agreement did not end the war in Vietnam, nor did the withdrawal of American troops. There was a cease-fire, but two years later, the North Vietnamese launched an offensive. They captured key areas, including Dong Xoai and Phuoc Long City. Even though the Paris peace agreement had been violated, there were no repercussions against North Vietnam.

The United States became consumed with its own crisis when a political scandal known as Watergate was uncovered. Numerous top government officials had been involved in illegal activities. President Nixon resigned on August 9, 1974, and Vice President Gerald Ford became the new president.

When North Vietnamese forces advanced on the central highlands area, nearly 60,000 South Vietnamese troops were killed. Afterward, the North Vietnamese captured the Quang Tri province. Within five weeks, the Northern armies captured twelve provinces with a population of eight million people. The end came as the North Vietnamese advanced toward Saigon. The U.S. military began quickly flying people out of Vietnam on April 29, 1975. In just 18 hours, over 1,000 Americans and 7,000 South Vietnamese left Vietnam.

The last two Americans to die in the Vietnam War were killed at 4:03 A.M. on April 30, 1975, during a rocket attack at the Saigon airport. Saigon fell that day as North Vietnamese forces captured the presidential palace. The marines guarding the American embassy were the last to leave as dawn lit the city, which would be renamed Ho Chi Minh City.

The war was over. Some called it the war in Indochina. Americans called it the Vietnam War. North Vietnamese called it the American War.

During Nixon's term, the war expanded into the neighboring countries of Laos and Cambodia as forces tried to locate Communist headquarters and supply routes. More than three times the number of bombs used in World

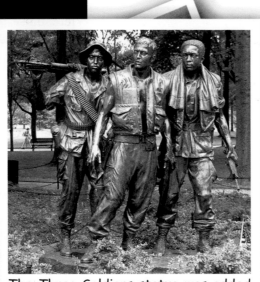

This more traditional sculpture, which is also known as *The Three Servicemen statue*, shows three soldiers with infantry weapons.

The Three Soldiers statue was added to the Vietnam Veterans Memorial in Washington, D.C., two years after The Wall was dedicated.

War II were dropped on Vietnam, Cambodia, and Laos during the Vietnam War. The many secret campaigns into these countries were investigated for violating international rights.

The Vietnam War holds the distinction of being the longest war that the United States has been involved in and the only one it ever lost. Military strategists have tried to analyze why. General Douglas Kinnard served in Vietnam and later wrote a book called *The War Managers* based on a questionnaire he sent to all the generals who served as combat commanders in Vietnam. To his surprise, two-thirds of the 173 generals filled out and returned their questionnaires. Kinnard wrote, "Probably the most startling thing to me was that almost seventy percent said they really didn't understand the war's objectives."[1]

The numbers were costly on all sides. Nearly a million North Vietnamese and Viet Cong troops and a quarter million South Vietnamese soldiers died. Hundreds of thousands of civilians had been killed; many more were homeless. After the war, North Vietnam held almost a million South Vietnamese in "reeducation camps," where most were kept for many years under harsh conditions. Vietnamese poet Nguyen Duy wrote, "In the end, in every war, whoever won, the people always lost."[2]

U.S. combat deaths in Vietnam exceeded the 33,629 men killed in the Korean War by April of 1969. By the end of the Vietnam War, there were 58,193 dead. Many of these were young men between eighteen and twenty-one years of age—youngsters who had been drafted. The wounded numbered more than 300,000; five thousand of those lost at least one limb.

The effects of the war continued long after the war ended. Although the U.S. Department of Agriculture banned the use of dioxin or Agent Orange in 1970, its use continued in Vietnam for three more years. Approximately 240 pounds of poison were sprayed on South Vietnam, destroying almost 2.5 million acres. A 1973 Harvard University study measured dioxin in the food, soil, and water in Vietnam. Measurements showed dioxin levels as high as 800 parts per trillion (50 parts per trillion was the upper limit for safe food). Today, the soil in Vietnam is much safer, except for areas around old American air bases. The Vietnamese also continue to be exposed to tear gas leaking from barrels into the ground and water.

The human costs have been even more significant. Vietnamese scientists linked Agent Orange to increased rates of digestive problems, neural disease, skin disease, and cancer. Women living in sprayed regions had increased pregnancy problems and children born with severe birth defects.

American soldiers were also exposed to Agent Orange. The U.S. Department of Veterans Affairs reported a higher-than-normal occurrence of certain cancers, peripheral neuropathy, and diabetes. Children of female veterans were at increased risk of birth defects. Spina bifida was a risk in children of all Vietnam veterans.

Pulitzer Prize–winning author Stanley Karnow reported: "A Veterans Administration survey released in 1988 estimated that some five hundred

Around 2.5 million people pay their respects at the Vietnam Veterans Memorial each year.

After a design contest, Maya Ying Lin's simple but powerful design of two granite walls was chosen for the Vietnam Veterans Memorial. The site is more commonly known as The Wall.

thousand of the three million U.S. troops who served in Vietnam suffered from 'post-traumatic stress disorder'—a higher percentage than those affected by 'shell shock' in World War I and 'battle fatigue' in World War II."[3] According to Karnow, the difference was that the danger soldiers faced in Vietnam was constant. There was no safe place to be in Vietnam.

One of the first things President Jimmy Carter did after taking office was pardon the men who had dodged the draft. He then signed legislation providing a site to honor Vietnam veterans, in Constitution Gardens near the Lincoln Memorial in Washington, D.C. In October 1980, the Vietnam Veterans Memorial Foundation announced a design contest. By the March 31, 1981, deadline, 1,421 design entries had been submitted. The winner of the contest was an undergraduate student at Yale University, Maya Ying Lin of Ohio. She was the daughter of Chinese parents who fled China in 1949 when the Communists came to power. Lin's idea was two walls that seemed to stretch to the Washington Monument in one direction and the Lincoln Memorial in the other. The walls would be made of polished black granite to reflect the trees and buildings in the distance.

Construction of the Vietnam Veterans Memorial began on March 16, 1982, and it was dedicated on November 13 of that year. The nine-million-dollar site known to many as "the Wall" was built entirely from private donations. Each wall is 246.75 feet long. Each end of the Wall seems to rise from the earth. The point where the walls meet is 10.1 feet high. As of 2005, there were 58,256 names engraved on the Wall, listed chronologically according to the date the person died or went missing. The first names, from 1959, and the last names, from 1975, meet in the center. The Vietnam Veterans Memorial is engraved with these words:

IN HONOR OF THE MEN AND WOMEN OF THE ARMED FORCES OF THE UNITED STATES WHO SERVED IN THE VIETNAM WAR. THE NAMES OF THOSE WHO GAVE THEIR LIVES AND OF THOSE WHO REMAIN MISSING ARE INSCRIBED IN THE ORDER THEY WERE TAKEN FROM US. OUR NATION HONORS THE COURAGE, SACRIFICE AND DEVOTION TO DUTY AND COUNTRY OF ITS VIETNAM VETERANS. THIS MEMORIAL WAS BUILT WITH PRIVATE CONTRIBUTIONS FROM THE AMERICAN PEOPLE. NOVEMBER 11, 1982.

Almost a million Vietnamese refugees have settled in the United States, making them the largest group of any Southeast Asian refugees in the country. After Saigon fell, about 135,000 Vietnamese fled to America. They were mainly military and government officials and their families. They first arrived at one of four U.S. military bases in California, Arkansas, Pennsylvania, and Florida. Social service agencies and the State Department resettled the refugees in communities throughout the country.

The immediate reunification of Vietnam wasn't entirely as successful as the new government had hoped it would be. Many Vietnamese of Chinese heritage were unwanted by the government. Thousands of families of farmers and fishermen left Vietnam by boat. The boats were often small and overcrowded and not meant to be sailed on rough ocean waters. It is estimated that almost half of these refugees drowned at sea.

The lucky ones made it to camps in Thailand, Malaysia, Indonesia, the Philippines, and Hong Kong. From those camps, many were allowed to leave for the United States or other countries. By the late 1970s, the United Nations High Commissioner for Refugees was able to negotiate an agreement with the government of Vietnam to allow Vietnamese with relatives in other countries to leave and join their families.

U.S. Marines evacuated refugees from Vietnam on April 29, 1975, taking them by helicopter to the USS *Blue Ridge*.

Another population of concern was the Amerasians, children born to Vietnamese women and American fathers during the war years. Because they were of "mixed blood," the Vietnamese government looked down on them. After the U.S. Congress passed a law allowing Amerasians to be admitted to the United States as immigrants, about 100,000 Amerasians immigrated.

By 2007, the largest number of Vietnamese in the United States were living in Southern California around the Los Angeles area. Other refugees have settled in the suburbs of Washington, D.C., and the two largest cities in Texas: Houston and Dallas. Other areas with large numbers of Vietnamese people are the states of Washington, Pennsylvania, Minnesota, Massachusetts, New York, and Illinois.

Chronology

1945   Ho Chi Minh declares independence for Vietnam and creates a provisional government.

1946   War begins between North Vietnam and France.

1950   The Chinese and Soviets offer weapons to the Viet Minh.

1954   French forces withdraw from Vietnam; the Geneva Accords provide for the temporary division of Vietnam along the seventeenth parallel.

1955   Ngo Dinh Diem becomes president of South Vietnam.

1962   U.S. military begins using Agent Orange.

1963   Buddhist monks set themselves on fire in opposition to Diem; Diem is overthrown.

1964   Gulf of Tonkin incident occurs in August and is followed by the Gulf of Tonkin Resolution.

1965   Operation Rolling Thunder is put into effect; first American combat troops arrive in Vietnam.

1968   Tet Offensive is launched on January 31; 200 civilians are killed in the My Lai massacre in March; Paris peace talks begin.

1969   Ho Chi Minh dies at the age of seventy-nine.

1971   The Pentagon Papers are published in the *New York Times*.

1972   U.S. planes bomb Hanoi and Haiphong in the "Christmas bombings."

1973   The Vietnam cease-fire agreement is signed in Paris in January; the first prisoners of war are released from Hanoi in February; the last American troops leave Vietnam on March 29.

1974   South Vietnamese President Thieu announces in January that war in Vietnam has resumed; Lieutenant William Calley is released on parole after serving one-third of his ten-year prison sentence for the My Lai massacre; the North Vietnamese begin attacks on the Phuoc Long province north of Saigon.

1975   North Vietnamese forces capture Phuoc Binh, the capital of Phuoc Long province, in January; Communists seize Saigon in April. Vietnam is unified by Vietnamese communists.

1982   The Vietnam Veterans Memorial in Washington, D.C., is dedicated.

1989   Vietnamese troops withdraw from Cambodia.

1995   Vietnam government promises to cooperate in finding all Americans still listed as missing. The U.S. restores diplomatic ties with Vietnam.

2000   President Bill Clinton becomes the first U.S. president to visit Vietnam since 1969.

2001   Vietnam and the United States enter into a trade agreement.

2004   First commercial air flight from the United States to Vietnam since the Vietnam War.

2005   In June, Prime Minister Phan Van Khai becomes the first Vietnamese leader to visit the United States since the end of the Vietnam War.

2007   Vietnam is admitted to the World Trade Organization. The U.S. agrees to fund a study on removing Agent Orange from Vietnam.

Timeline in History

1917–1918	United States fights in World War I.
1929	American stock market crashes, beginning the Great Depression.
1941	United States enters World War II after bombing of Hawaii's Pearl Harbor.
1945	U.S. warplanes drop atomic bombs on Japan; Japan surrenders. President Franklin D. Roosevelt dies.
1949	North Atlantic Treaty Organization (NATO) is formed.
1950	President Harry Truman sends U.S. troops to Korea.
1954	U.S. Senate condemns Senator Joseph McCarthy for Communist "witch hunt."
1960	John F. Kennedy is elected president.
1963	Martin Luther King Jr. delivers "I have a dream" speech. Kennedy is assassinated on November 22; Vice President Lyndon B. Johnson becomes president.
1964	Lyndon B. Johnson is elected president.
1968	Martin Luther King Jr. and Robert Kennedy are assassinated. Rioting erupts at Democratic National Convention in Chicago; Richard Nixon is elected president.
1970	Student protesters are killed by National Guardsmen at Kent State University.
1972	Richard Nixon is reelected.
1973	Former President Johnson dies at his home in Texas. Watergate hearings begin in June.
1974	The House Judiciary Committee recommends impeachment proceedings against President Nixon. In August, Richard Nixon resigns as president of the United States; Vice President Gerald R. Ford is sworn in as president.
1976	Jimmy Carter is elected president and pardons draft dodgers.
1980	Ronald Reagan is elected president.
1982	United States invades Grenada.
1988	George H. W. Bush is elected president.
1991	The United States fights in the Gulf War; the Soviet Union dissolves.
1992	Bill Clinton is elected president.
2000	George W. Bush is elected president.
2001	Middle Eastern terrorists fly commercial airplanes into the Pentagon and World Trade Center on September 11.
2002	United States enters war in Iraq.
2004	First cases of human death as a result from bird flu occurs in Vietnam. An earthquake occurs in the Indian Ocean on December 26, setting off tsunamis that destroy many communities throughout Southeast Asia. Over 200,000 people die or are declared missing.
2006	National Marine Corp Museum opens at Quantico on Veteran's Day.
2007	The International Olympic Committee decides that the former Communist country of Russia will host the Winter Olympics in 2014.

Chapter Notes

Chapter 1
Surprise Attack
1. *The New York Times,* "Embassy Attack: A Fight to Death," February 1, 1968, p. 14.
2. Charles Mohr, *The New York Times,* "Foe Invades U.S. Saigon Embassy," January 31, 1968, p. 2.
3. Stanley Karnow, *Vietnam: A History* (New York: Penguin, 1983), p. 542.
4. Christian G. Appy, *Patriots: The Vietnam War Remembered from All Sides* (New York: Viking, 2003), p. 296.
5. Ibid., p. 261.
6. Karnow, p. 536.

Chapter 2
Vietnam Seeks Independence
1. Christian G. Appy, *Patriots: The Vietnam War Remembered from All Sides* (New York: Viking, 2003), p. 36.
2. Ibid., p. 63.
3. Ibid., p. 68.
4. Ibid., p. 139.
5. Ibid., p. 66.
6. "Report from Vietnam," Walter Cronkite Broadcast, February 27, 1968, http://www.alvernia.edu/cgi-bin/mt/text/archives/000194.html

Chapter 3
Americans Join the War in Vietnam
1. Christian G. Appy, *Patriots: The Vietnam War Remembered from All Sides* (New York: Viking, 2003), p. 200.
2. Ibid., p. 171.

Chapter 4
How to End a War
1. *The New York Times,* "Waste Them," April 15, 1970, p. 42.
2. Christian G. Appy, *Patriots: The Vietnam War Remembered from All Sides* (New York: Viking, 2003), p. 63.
3. *The New York Times,* "The Covert War," June 13, 1971, p. 38.

Chapter 5
Aftermath
1. Christian G. Appy, *Patriots: The Vietnam War Remembered from All Sides* (New York: Viking, 2003), p. 321.
2. Ibid., p. 257.
3. Stanley Karnow, *Vietnam: A History* (New York: Penguin, 1983), p. 33.

Further Reading

For Young Adults

Levy, Debbie. *The Vietnam War: Chronicle of America's Wars.* Minneapolis: Lerner Publications, 2004.

Willoughby, Douglas. *The Vietnam War.* Chicago: Heinemann Library, 2001.

Yancey, Diane. *Life of an American Soldier in Vietnam.* San Diego, California: Lucent Books, 2001.

Works Consulted

Appy, Christian G. *Patriots: The Vietnam War Remembered from All Sides.* New York: Viking, 2003.

"The Covert War." *The New York Times,* June 13, 1971, p. 38.

Ellsberg, Daniel. *Secrets: A Memoir of Vietnam and the Pentagon Papers.* New York: Viking, 2002.

"Embassy Attack: A Fight to Death." *The New York Times,* February 1, 1968, p. 14.

Goldman, Peter, and Tony Fuller. *Charlie Company: What Vietnam Did to Us.* New York: William Morrow, 1983.

Karnow, Stanley. *Vietnam: A History.* New York: Penguin, 1983.

Maclear, Michael. *The Ten Thousand Day War: Vietnam: 1945–1975.* New York: St. Martin's Press, 1981.

Mohr, Charles. "Foe Invades U.S. Saigon Embassy." *The New York Times,* January 31, 1968, pp. 1–2.

"Waste Them." *The New York Times,* April 15, 1970, p. 42.

Welsh, Douglas. *The History of the Vietnam War.* New York: Galahad Books, 1982.

On the Internet

The New York Times on the Web Learning Network: *The Fall of Saigon* http://www.nytimes.com/learning/general/specials/saigon

PBS: *American Experience: Vietnam Online* http://www.pbs.org/wgbh/amex/vietnam

PBS: *Battlefield Vietnam* http://www.pbs.org/battlefieldvietnam

PBS: *RE: Vietnam: Stories Since the War* http://www.pbs.org/pov/stories

Vietnam Veterans Memorial Fund http://www.vvmf.org/

The Vietnam Veterans Memorial Wall Page http://thewall-usa.com

VietnamWar.net: *Educational, Entertainment, and Research Material Relevant to the Study of the Vietnam War* http://www.vietnamwar.net

Glossary

ambush (AAM-bush)—to hide and then attack someone.

autonomous (aw-TAH-nuh-mus)—self-governing.

battalion (buh-TAAL-yun)—a large unit of soldiers.

civilian (sih-VIL-yun)—someone who is not a member of the armed forces.

cold war (KOHLD WAR)—a dispute between Eastern and Western countries during the last half of the twentieth century. It did not involve military battles.

colonialism (kuh-LOH-nee-ul-iz-um)—the policy of acquiring or maintaining a distant land.

embassy (EM-buh-see)—the official place in a foreign country where an ambassador lives and works.

fortified (FOR-tuh-fyd)—made stronger against attack.

guerrilla (guh-RIH-luh)—a member of a small group of fighters or soldiers who often launch surprise attacks against an official army.

hamlet (HAAM-let)—a very small village.

herbicide (ER-bih-syd)—a substance that is poisonous to plants.

infiltrated (IN-fil-tray-ted)—joined an enemy's side secretly in order to spy or cause some sort of damage.

malaria (muh-LAYR-ee-uh)—an often fatal disease spread by mosquitoes.

martial (MAR-shul)—related to war or soldiers.

nationalism (NAA-shuh-nul-iz-um)—loyalty to and pride in one's nation or country.

provincial (proh-VIN-shul)—related to a province or part of a country.

refugee (ref-yoo-JEE *or* REF-yoo-jee)—a person who is forced to leave his or her home because of war, persecution, or natural disaster.

repercussions (ree-pur-KUH-shuns)—indirect effects or reactions.

retaliate (ree-TAAL-ee-ayt)—to do something unpleasant to someone because the person has done something unpleasant to you.

silhouette (sil-oo-ET)—a dark outline seen against a light background.

Index